Volume 68 of the Yale Series of Younger Poets

Field
Guide

ROBERT HASS

NEW HAVEN AND LONDON, YALE UNIVERSITY PRESS, 1973

Published with assistance from
the Mary Cady Tew Memorial Fund.

Library of Congress catalog card number: 72–91296
ISBN: 0–300–01650–6 (cloth), 0–300–01651–4 (paper)

Designed by Sally Sullivan
and set in Monotype Aldine Bembo type
by The Stinehour Press, Lunenburg, Vt.
Printed in the United States of America by
The Colonial Press, Inc., Clinton, Mass.

Published in Great Britain, Europe, and Africa by
Yale University Press, Ltd., London.
Distributed in Canada by McGill–Queen's University
Press, Montreal; in Latin America by Kaiman & Polon,
Inc., New York City; in Australasia and Southeast
Asia by John Wiley & Sons Australasia Pty. Ltd.,
Sydney; In India by UBS Publishers' Distributors Pvt.,
Ltd., Delhi; in Japan by John Weatherhill, Inc., Tokyo.

For Earlene, Leif, Kristin, Luke,
and for friends

Contents

In Weather

Acknowledgments

Acknowledgment is made to the following publications
for poems which originally appeared in them.

Antaeus: "Fall," "Spring," "Song," "Two Views of
  Buson," "The Return of Robinson Jeffers"
Choice: "Letter," "Lament for the Poles of Buffalo"
The Hudson Review: "On the Coast near Sausalito,"
  "Bookbuying in the Tenderloin," "Concerning the
  Afterlife, the Indians of Central California Had Only
  the Dimmest Notions," "The Pornographer," "The
  Pornographer, Melancholy," "The Pornographer at
  the End of Winter," "Politics of a Pornographer"
The Nation: "Black Mountain, Los Altos"
Rapport: "Maps," "The Nineteenth Century as a
  Song," "In Weather"
Poetry: "San Pedro Road," "Lines on Last Spring,"
  "The Failure of Buffalo to Levitate"
Salmagundi: "Graveyard at Bolinas," "Palo Alto: The
  Marshes," "After I Seized the Pentagon"
The Young American Poets (Chicago: Follett, 1968):
  "Letter to a Poet," "Adhesive: For Earlene"

The author wishes to thank Robert Duncan for
  permission to reprint a line from *The Opening of the
  Field* (New York: Grove Press, 1960) in "Letter."
The versions of Japanese poems depend absolutely on
  R. H. Blyth's great *Haiku* (Tokyo: Hokuseido Press,
  1949–52).

Foreword

Some poems present themselves as cliffs that need to be climbed. Others are so defensive that when you approach their enclosure you half expect to be met by a snarling dog at the gate. Still others want to smother you with their sticky charms. Reading a poem by Robert Hass is like stepping into the ocean when the temperature of the water is not much different from that of the air. You scarcely know, until you feel the undertow tug at you, that you have entered into another element. Suddenly the deep is there, with its teeming life.

Consider the opening lines of "On the Coast near Sausalito":

> I won't say much for the sea
> except that it was, almost,
> the color of sour milk.
> The sun in that clear
> unmenacing sky was low,
> angled off the grey fissure of the cliffs,
> hills dark green with manzanita.

It was as if the voice were the continuation of a long soliloquy that had only just now become audible, without straining to be heard, without breathing harder—a clear musical voice that modulates itself as it flows and that enjoys caressing the long vowel sounds.

Later in the poem we are introduced to "an ugly atavistic fish," the cabezone, a variety of Pacific sculpin that with its duck's-web fins and bloated head "resembles a prehistoric toad." It belongs to the category of trash fish, but Italians prize it for the savor of its bluish meat when fried in olive oil "with a sprig of fresh rosemary." (Hass is characteristically explicit with his culinary instructions.)

At the close of the poem the fisherman confronts his squirming catch, that "spiny monster" held in his hands:

> his bulging purple eyes
> were eyes and the sun was
> almost tangent to the planet
> on our uneasy coast.
> Creature and creature,
> we stared down centuries.

Hass's poetry is permeated with the awareness of his creature self, his affinity with the animal and vegetable kingdoms, with the whole chain of being. The country from which he has his passport is the natural universe, to which he pledges his imagination. He is most at home writing of his native Pacific coast, but he carries his passport with him wherever he goes. Natural universe and moral universe coincide for him, centered in a nexus of personal affections, his stay against what he describes as "the wilderness of history and political violence." For one so caring, an occasional lapse into sentimentality would be understandable, but a reliable sense of humor and a certain aspect of down-to-earth plainness in his makeup prevent him from going soft. He does not, for example, break into tears over the sufferings of his skillet-bound cabezone: it is enough that he has transformed its ugliness into beauty and dignified its fate in the act of confrontation. To a troubled friend in another poem he remarks, "This world did not invite us."

In his mid-twenties, for an anthology of young poets, Hass composed a brief statement of poetics that remains revealing: "I like poems for the peace involved in reading and writing them. I began writing seriously when I found that I could write about myself and the world I knew,

San Francisco and the country around it, in a fairly simple and direct way. For a long time I felt a compulsion to direct myself to large issues; this was mainly due to the cant I acquired around universities about alienation. About the time that the Vietnam War broke out, it became clear to me that alienation was a state approaching to sanity, a way of being human in a monstrously inhuman world, and that feeling human was a useful form of political subversion."*

The shapes of evil in his poems are identifiable as spoilers and predators; inheritors of "the old fury of land grants, maps, and deeds of trust"; robber barons east and west; warmongers and bigots. In "Palo Alto: The Marshes" Kit Carson is glimpsed anticipating the rape of California with the torch he puts to an Indian village, a vision mounted on the apparition of "ten wagonloads of fresh-caught salmon" and dissolving to the harsh reality of a tanker lugging "bomb-shaped napalm tins toward port at Redwood City," site of the chemical factory whose business is with death by fire. "Palo Alto: The Marshes" is a brilliant and profound poem of American history. Its ending, with its crystalline detail and authority of tone—remarkable in a poet so young—typifies Hass's style at its best:

> The otters are gone from the bay
> and I have seen five horses
> easy in the grassy marsh
> beside three snowy egrets.
>
> Bird cries and the unembittered sun,
> wings and the white bodies of the birds,
> it is morning. Citizens are rising
> to murder in their moral dreams.

* Paul Carroll, ed., *The Young American Poets* (Chicago: Follett, 1968).

At first glance Hass appears to be an expansive poet in the open tradition of Walt Whitman and William Carlos Williams; but gradually we perceive his attachment to more private imaginations, including those of Wallace Stevens and Theodore Roethke. Some of the energy of his writing can be attributed to the contradictions of this ancestral line. An added element is the influence on his work of Chinese and Japanese poetry, evident in the scrupulous purity of his observation—as in the ending of "Song," one of the most buoyant and delightful of his lyrics:

> On the oak table
> filets of sole
> stewing in the juice of tangerines,
> slices of green pepper
> on a bone-white dish.

Hass's debt to the Orient is acknowledged in the sequence entitled "After the Gentle Poet Kobayashi Issa," based on the standard haiku translations by R. H. Blyth. A comparison of texts may serve to indicate the extent of Hass's stylistic accomplishment. Blyth's version of the eighth haiku reads:

> Spiders in the corners,
> Don't worry!
> I'm not going to sweep them.

Hass's transpositions and modifications are subtle:

> Don't worry, spiders,
> I keep house
> casually.

The exquisite differences are what make poetry.

Eastern influence is only one of the factors contributing to the particularity of Hass's style. The underlying assumptions are inherently philosophical. Was it Sartre who said, "Evil is making abstract that which is concrete"?

Haiku and other poems of literary reference are gathered in the middle of *Field Guide* under the heading "A Pencil." Included in this group is a series of "pornographer poems," as if to underscore the bond between sexuality and art. Presumably the section heading has Freudian connotations, though its origin is innocent enough. Faulkner, it seems, was once asked by an interviewer what it took to be a writer. "A pencil," he replied. It will be recalled that Renoir, in his arthritic age, when he could scarcely lift his hand, employed a blunter term to designate his painting tool. My favorite in this section is "The Nineteenth Century as a Song," a witty tour de force—but it is only slightly pornographic.

Two of Hass's most ambitious poems, "In Weather" and "Lament for the Poles of Buffalo," considered in conjunction, display the versatility of his gifts. The former is that rare contemporary phenomenon, a testimony to the persistence of married love through a long winter and the metamorphoses of the heart. Hass already knows what it took Pound a lifetime to learn: "If love be not in the house there is nothing" (Canto 116). "In Weather" is intimate, reflective, tortuous, sensuous, a compulsive journey through the labyrinth of landscape into the mystery of affections:

> o spider cunt, o raw devourer.
> I wondered what to make
> of myself. There had been a thaw.
> I looked for green shoots
> in the garden, wild flowers in the woods.
> I found none.
> . . . .
> I could not sleep.
> I imagined the panic

of the meadow mouse,
the star-nosed mole.
Slowly at first, I
made a solemn face
and tried the almost human wail
of owls, ecstatic
in the winter trees, *twoo, twoo.*
I drew long breaths.
My wife stirred in our bed.
Joy seized me.

In contrast, "Lament for the Poles of Buffalo" is a public poem with a documentary base, dense with allusions to the local history of upper New York State, agitated and propelled by the thrust of current affairs. It is the most topical of Hass's poems, and the one best served by a commentary. A note on its background will illuminate many of its details.

In 1970, at the time of the Cambodian escalation, Hass was faculty adviser—an entirely titular position—to SDS (Students for a Democratic Society) at the State University of New York at Buffalo. In this capacity he was subpoenaed by the grand jury convened to investigate antiwar activity on the campus. At one level this is a poem of civic conscience, an outcry of sorrow and dismay, complicated by the irony of the poet's investiture as a leader of mad bombers and subversives. At another, more meditative level it is a probing for the meaning of roots in a deracinated community, by a man who is himself cut off, at least temporarily, from his Pacific source as well as from the mainstream of the national will.

"I had been teaching in the night school," he recalls, in a letter that is as informative as it is casual. His students were "Polish working class people who lived on streets named after poets and revolutionaries they had never heard of, ashamed of their nationality, some of the younger ones speaking very affectedly because they were trying to get rid of the whine in their vowels. There are not even Polish restaurants in the city, not one Polish bookstore. After San Francisco it was puzzling to me at first. I started teaching Polish books and they didn't like the idea at all. By the end we were trying out the Lithuanian salads in *Pan Tadeusz*. I was getting mason jars of their grandmothers' sauerkraut and in one case directions to a stretch of woods that held a treasure of birch mushrooms. . . ."

Robert Hass is a poet who sits easy in his skin. One is not accustomed to encounter, in the work of a contemporary, this much élan, this much celebration of "the quick pulse of blood." Almost every page demonstrates, with singular clarity, the satisfactions of an art committed to making "felt connections" between words and body, between body and world. These poems are as much an expression of an organic principle as the activities of which they are an extension—walking, eating, sleeping, lovemaking—and they are equally pleasurable, equally real. *Field Guide* is an event as much as it is literature.

> It is an ancient
> imagination and it begets,
> this order with the random symmetries
> of mallow poppies in the field,
> the dying and green leafing of the grass,
> meadows crackling in the midday heat,
> alive with seed. It translates easily.

STANLEY KUNITZ

The Coast

On the Coast near Sausalito

1

I won't say much for the sea
except that it was, almost,
the color of sour milk.
The sun in that clear
unmenacing sky was low,
angled off the grey fissure of the cliffs,
hills dark green with manzanita.

Low tide: slimed rocks
mottled brown and thick with kelp
like the huge backs of ancient tortoises
merged with the grey stone
of the breakwater, sliding off
to antediluvian depths.
The old story: here filthy life begins.

2

Fish–
ing, as Melville said,
"to purge the spleen,"
to put to task my clumsy hands
my hands that bruise by
not touching
pluck the legs from a prawn,
peel the shell off,
and curl the body twice about a hook.

3

The cabezone is not highly regarded
by fishermen, except Italians
who have the grace
to fry the pale, almost bluish flesh
in olive oil with a sprig
of fresh rosemary.

The cabezone, an ugly atavistic fish,
as old as the coastal shelf
it feeds upon
has fins of duck's-web thickness,
resembles a prehistoric toad,
and is delicately sweet.

Catching one, the fierce quiver of surprise
and the line's tension
are a recognition.

4

But it's strange to kill
for the sudden feel of life.
The danger is
to moralize
that strangeness.
Holding the spiny monster in my hands
his bulging purple eyes
were eyes and the sun was
almost tangent to the planet
on our uneasy coast.
Creature and creature,
we stared down centuries.

Fall

Amateurs, we gathered mushrooms
near shaggy eucalyptus groves
which smelled of camphor and the fog-soaked earth.
Chanterelles, puffballs, chicken-of-the-woods,
we cooked in wine or butter,
beaten eggs or sour cream,
half expecting to be
killed by a mistake. "Intense perspiration,"
you said late at night,
quoting the terrifying field guide
while we lay tangled in our sheets and heavy limbs,
"is the first symptom of attack."

Friends called our aromatic fungi
"liebestoads" and only ate the ones
that we most certainly survived.
Death shook us more than once
those days and floating back
it felt like life. Earth-wet, slithery,
we drifted toward the names of things.
Spore prints littered our table
like nervous stars. Rotting caps
gave off a musky smell of loam.

Black Mountain, Los Altos

Clumps of ghostly buckeye
       bleached bones
weirdly grey in the runoff
between ridges, the flats
in fog. Five deer grazing
on the long hill, the soft
cluck of mourning doves,
creeks running. I feel
furry as sage here
after an hour's walk
in clear midmorning air.
                     Only
three species of tree in
all these hills: blue oak,
buckeye, and patches of
wind-rasped laurel.
In the old quiet the Indians
could have heard bells
at Mission Santa Clara
where the brown-cowled padres
taught the sorrowful mysteries
with a whip. They
manufacture napalm
in the fog where Redwood
City sprawls into the bay.
I think of the village
of Bien Hoa, the early spring
death in the buckeyes
and up the long valley
my eyes flash, another
knife, clean as malice.

Maps

Sourdough french bread and pinot chardonnay

*

Apricots—
the downy buttock shape
hard black sculpture of the limbs
on Saratoga hillsides in the rain.

*

These were the staples of the China trade:
sea otter, sandalwood, and bêche-de-mer

*

The pointillist look of laurels
their dappled pale green body stirs
down valley in the morning wind
Daphne was supple
my wife is tan, blue-rippled
pale in the dark hollows

*

Kit Carson in California:
it was the eyes of fish
that shivered in him the tenderness of eyes
he watched the ships come in
at Yerba Buena once, found obscene
the intelligence of crabs
their sidelong crawl, gulls
screeching for white meat
flounders in tubs, startled

*

Musky fall—
slime of a saffron milkcap
the mottled amanita
delicate phallic toxic

*

How odd
the fruity warmth of zinfandel
geometries of "rational viticulture"

*

   Plucked from algae sea spray
cold sun and a low rank tide
   sea cucumbers
lolling in the crevices of rock
they traded men enough
to carve old Crocker's railway out of rock
to eat these slugs
bêche-de-mer

*

The night they bombed Hanoi
we had been drinking red pinot
that was winter the walnut tree was bare
and the desert ironwood where waxwings
perched in spring drunk on pyracantha

squalls headwinds days gone
north on the infelicitous Pacific

*

The bleak intricate erosion of these cliffs

   seas grown bitter
with the salt of continents

*

Jerusalem artichokes
raised on sandy bluffs at San Gregorio
near reedy beaches where the steelhead ran

Coast range runoff turned salt creek
in the heat and indolence of August

*

That purple in the hills
    owl's clover stiffening the lupine
while the white flowers of the pollinated plant
    seep red

the eye owns what is familiar
    felt along the flesh
"an amethystine tinge"

*

Chants, recitations:
Olema
Tamalpais Mariposa
Mendocino Sausalito San Rafael
Emigrant Gap
Donner Pass

Of all the laws
that bind us to the past
the names of things are
stubbornest

*

Late summer—
red berries darken the hawthorns
curls of yellow in the laurels

your body and the undulant
sharp edges of the hills

*

Clams, abalones, cockles, chitons, crabs

*

Ishi
in San Francisco, 1911:
it was not the sea he wondered at
that inland man who saw the salmon
die to spawn and fed his dwindling people
from their rage to breed
it was the thousands of white bodies
on the beach
"Hansi saltu . . ." so many
ghosts

*

The long ripple in the swamp grass
is a skunk
he shuns the day

Adhesive: For Earlene

How often we overslept
those grey enormous mornings
in the first year of marriage
and found that rain and wind
had scattered palm nuts,
palm leaves, and sweet rotting crabapples
across our wildered lawn.

By spring your belly was immense
and your coloring a high rosy almond.

We were so broke
we debated buying thumbtacks
at the Elmwood Dime Store
knowing cellophane tape would do.
Berkeley seemed more innocent
in those flush days
when we skipped lunch
to have the price of *Les Enfants de Paradis.*

Letter to a Poet

A mockingbird leans
from the walnut, bellies,
riffling white, accomplishes

his perch upon the eaves.
I witnessed this act of grace
in blind California

in the January sun
where families bicycle on Saturday
and the mother with high cheekbones

and coffee-colored iridescent
hair curses her child
in the language of Pushkin—

John, I am dull from
thinking of your pain,
this mimic world

which makes us stupid
with the totem griefs
we hope will give us

power to look at trees,
at stones, one brute to another
like poems on a page.

What can I say, my friend?
There are tricks of animal grace,
poems in the mind

we survive on. It isn't much.
You are 4,000 miles away &
this world did not invite us.

Bookbuying in the Tenderloin

A statuary Christ bleeds sweating grief
in the Gethsemane garden of St. Boniface Church
where empurpled Irish winos lurch
to their salvation. When incense and belief
will not suffice: ruby port in the storm
of muscatel-made images of hell
the city spews at their shuffling feet.
In the Longshoremen's Hall across the street,
three decades have unloaded since the fight
to oust the manic Trotskyite
screwballs from the brotherhood. All goes well
since the unions closed their ranks,
boosted their pensions, and hired the banks
to manage funds for the workingman's cartel.
Christ in plaster, the unions minting coin,
old hopes converge upon the Tenderloin
where Comte, Considerant, Fourier
are thick with dust in the two-bit tray
of cavernous secondhand bookstores
and the streets suffuse the ten-cent howl
of jukebox violence, just this side of blues.
Negro boy-whores in black tennis shoes
prowl in front of noisy hustler bars.
Like Samuel Gompers, they want more
on this street where every other whore
is painfully skinny, wears a bouffant,
and looks like a brown slow-blooming annual flower.
In the places that I haunt, no power
to transform the universal squalor

nor wisdom to withstand the thin wrists
of the girls who sell their bodies for a dollar
or two, the price of a Collected Maeterlinck.
The sky glowers. My God, it is a test,
this riding out the dying of the West.

Spring

We bought great ornamental oranges,
Mexican cookies, a fragrant yellow tea.
Browsed the bookstores. You
asked mildly, "Bob, who is Ugo Betti?"
A bearded bird-like man
(he looked like a Russian priest
with imperial bearing
and a black ransacked raincoat)
turned to us, cleared
his cultural throat, and
told us both interminably
who Ugo Betti was. The slow
filtering of sun through windows
glazed to gold the silky hair
along your arms. Dusk was
a huge weird phosphorescent beast
dying slowly out across the bay.
Our house waited and our books,
the skinny little soldiers on the shelves.
After dinner I read one anyway.
You chanted, "Ugo Betti has no bones,"
and when I said, "The limits of my language
are the limits of my world," you laughed.
We spoke all night in tongues,
in fingertips, in teeth.

Graveyard at Bolinas

Yews as tall as pines
and lonelier
lean to the weather there
dark against the sky.
Gulls hover,
herons ride the wind
across the bluff,
their great wings wide.

The markers are scattered like teeth
or bones among wild violets
and reedy onion grass:
Eliab Streeter,
Gamaliel St. John.
At the end of their world
these transplanted Yankees
put down roots at last
and give a sour fragrance to the air.

Sarah Ransom,
all her days an upright wife.

Velorous Hodge,
done with the slaughtering of seals.

In the shadow of a peeling eucalyptus
Eliza Granger Binns is

"With Christ, which is better"
(1852–1858).

The delicate
light green leaves of monkey flowers
(or Indian lettuce)
are tangled on her grave
in thick small curls.
I picked a bunch
thinking to make
a salad of Eliza Binns.

Afterwards I walked along the beach,
remembering how the oldest markers,
glazed by sea wind,
were effaced, clean
as driftwood, incurious
as stone. The sun was on my neck.
Some days it's not so hard to say
the quick pulse of blood
through living flesh
is all there is.

At Stinson Beach

Trompe l'oeil stillness in a steady rain

The coast road: morning glories in a drainage ditch
Pale touch-me-nots: suicide in early spring,
Its particular agony, the false note

By what name, when blossom
Falls on blossom, rain
On rain

What she brought back from that minute tranquillity
She never said

How the flower of her body
Danced her dresses into light

Fog and the early sun, an easy wind
She danced swaying in the stalled light
She danced easily without occasion

Variations in green, ferns, redwood, the rain

San Pedro Road

Casting, up a salt creek in the sea-rank air,
fragrance of the ferny anise, crackle of field grass
in the summer heat. Under this sun vision blurs.
Blue air rises, the horizon weaves above the leaden bay.
Rock crabs scuttle from my shadow in the silt.

Some other day the slow-breathing, finely haired mussels
on the shore, under rocks, buried thick-clustered in
    black mud
would be enough, blended in a quick formal image
with butter, tarragon, a cool white Napa Valley wine.
Today in the ferocious pointless heat I dream,
half in anger, of the great white bass,
the curious striper, bright-eyed, rising to the bait,
flickering in muddy bottoms, feeding the green
brackish channels where yachts wallow in the windless air.
My hands are tense.
                    A carcass washes by, white meat,
spidery translucent bones and I think I understand,
finally dumb animal I understand, kick off boots,
    pants, socks,
and swim,
            thrashing dull water to a golden brown,
terrorizing the depths with my white belly, my
    enormous length,
done with casting, reeling in slowly, casting . . .

Song

Afternoon cooking in the fall sun—
who is more naked
                                    than the man
yelling, "Hey, I'm home!"
                        to an empty house?
thinking because the bay is clear,
the hills in yellow heat,
& scrub oak red in gullies
                that great crowds of family
should tumble from the rooms
                        to throw their bodies on the Papa-body,
                                    I-am-loved.

Cat sleeps in the windowgleam,
                        dust motes.
    On the oak table
    filets of sole
stewing in the juice of tangerines,
    slices of green pepper
                on a bone-white dish.

Lines on Last Spring

for John Peck

1

I have been thinking again
of your acacia grove. Spring
had made a small start
in the meadow mushroom
and the flowering plum. Fog
heaved inland from the sea,
grey as the distances I feared
once falling into, driving east.
Your creek ran with new rain.

2

A clean taste for bitter things,
unripe almonds or hard words.
I touched the cold surfaces of rock
and peeled the roughened bark
from pepper trees. The air was thick
with birds, linnets like wounds,
slow towhees, dumb earth-colored birds,
hawks overhead riding in the wind.
The eucalyptus leaves we crumbled
smelled of pungent lemon in our hands.

3

We sucked at oranges we stole
from your alcoholic neighbors
who fermented in their bed
all day and watched TV.
Texas oil and California land
married their tanned, torpid bodies
and produced one hand steady enough
to switch the channels by remote control.
Clouds scudded in their great bay window
on the hill. Their hounds howled from the kennels
and hurled themselves against the fence.

4

We talked about the war,
examined tiers of pearl-
tinged fungi on a rotting pine
and, wryly, without conviction,
invented a small country
named Clarity or Passion
just north of Mendocino on the coast.

Palo Alto: The Marshes

For Mariana Richardson (1830–1891)

1

She dreamed along the beaches of this coast.
Here where the tide rides in to desolate
the sluggish margins of the bay,
sea grass sheens copper into distances.
Walking, I recite the hard
explosive names of birds:
egret, killdeer, bittern, tern.
Dull in the wind and early morning light,
the striped shadows of the cattails
twitch like nerves.

2

Mud, roots, old cartridges, and blood.
High overhead, the long silence of the geese.

3

"We take no prisoners," John Fremont said
and took California for President Polk.
That was the Bear Flag War.
She watched it from the Mission San Rafael,
named for the archangel (the terrible one)
who gently laid a fish across the eyes
of saintly, miserable Tobias
that he might see.
The eyes of fish. The land
shimmers fearfully.
No archangels here, no ghosts,
and terns rise like seafoam
from the breaking surf.

4

Kit Carson's antique .45, blue,
new as grease. The roar
flings up echoes,
row on row of shrieking avocets.
The blood of Francisco de Haro,
Ramon de Haro, José de los Reyes Berryessa
runs darkly to the old ooze.

5

The star thistles: erect, surprised,

6

and blooming
violet caterpillar hairs. One
of the de Haros was her lover,
the books don't say which.
They were twins.

7

In California in the early spring
there are pale yellow mornings
when the mist burns slowly into day.
The air stings
like autumn, clarifies
like pain.

8

Well I have dreamed this coast myself.
Dreamed Mariana, since her father owned the land
where I grew up. I saw her picture once:
a wraith encased in a high-necked black silk
dress so taut about the bones there were hardly ripples
for the light to play in. I knew her eyes
had watched the hills seep blue with lupine after rain,
seen the young peppers, heavy and intent,

first rosy drupes and then the acrid fruit,
the ache of spring. Black as her hair
the unreflecting venom of those eyes
is an aftermath I know, like these brackish,
russet pools a strange life feeds in
or the old fury of land grants, maps,
and deeds of trust. A furious dun-
colored mallard knows my kind
and skims across the edges of the marsh
where the dead bass surface
and their flaccid bellies bob.

9

A chill tightens the skin
around my bones. The other California
and its bitter absent ghosts
dance to a stillness in the air:
the Klamath tribe was routed and they disappeared.
Even the dust seemed stunned,
tools on the ground, fishnets.
Fires crackled, smouldering.
No movement but the slow turning
of the smoke, no sound but jays
shrill in the distance and flying further off.
The flicker of lizards, dragonflies.
And beyond the dry flag-woven lodges
a faint persistent slapping.
Carson found ten wagonloads
of fresh-caught salmon, silver
in the sun. The flat eyes stared.
Gills sucked the thin annulling air.
They flopped and shivered,
ten wagonloads. Kit Carson
burned the village to the ground.
They rode some twenty miles that day
and still they saw the black smoke
smear the sky above the pines.

10

Here everything seems clear,
firmly etched against the pale
smoky sky: sedge, flag, owl's clover,
rotting wharves. A tanker lugs silver
bomb-shaped napalm tins toward
port at Redwood City. Again,
my eye performs
the lobotomy of description.
Again, almost with yearning,
I see the malice of her ancient eyes.
The mud flats hiss as the tide turns.
They say she died in Redwood City,
cursing "the goddamned Anglo-Yankee yoke."

11

The otters are gone from the bay
and I have seen five horses
easy in the grassy marsh
beside three snowy egrets.

Bird cries and the unembittered sun,
wings and the white bodies of the birds,
it is morning. Citizens are rising
to murder in their moral dreams.

Concerning the Afterlife, the Indians of Central California Had Only the Dimmest Notions

It is morning because the sun has risen.

I wake slowly in the early heat,
   pick berries from the thorny vines.
   They are deep red,
   sugar-heavy, fuzzed with dust.
The eucalyptus casts a feathered shadow
on the house which gradually withdraws.

   After breakfast
you will swim and I am going to read
that hard man Thomas Hobbes
on the causes of the English civil wars.
There are no women in his world,
Hobbes, brothers fighting brothers
over goods.
               I see you in the later afternoon
your hair dry-yellow, plaited
from the waves, a faint salt sheen
across your belly and along your arms.
The kids bring from the sea
   intricate calcium gifts—
   black turbans, angular green whelks,
   the whorled opalescent unicorn.

We may or may not
feel some irritation at the dinner hour.
The first stars, and after dark
Vega hangs in the lyre,
the Dipper tilts above the hill.
                              Traveling
in Europe Hobbes was haunted by motion.
Sailing or riding, he was suddenly aware
that all things move.
                    We will lie down,
finally, in our heaviness
    and touch and drift toward morning.

A Pencil

The Nineteenth Century as a Song

"How like a well-kept garden is your soul."
   John Gray's translation of Verlaine
& Baudelaire's butcher in 1861
shorted him four centimes
on a pound of tripe.
He thought himself a clever man
and, wiping the calves' blood from his beefy hands,
gazed briefly at what Tennyson called
"the sweet blue sky."

It was a warm day.
What clouds there were
were made of sugar tinged with blood.
They shed, faintly, amid the clatter of carriages
new settings of the songs
Moravian virgins sang on wedding days.

   The poet is a monarch of the clouds

& Swinburne on his northern coast
"trod," he actually wrote, "by no tropic foot,"
composed that lovely elegy
and then found out Baudelaire was still alive
whom he had lodged dreamily
in a "deep division of prodigious breasts."

   Surely the poet is monarch of the clouds.
   He hovers, like a lemon-colored kite,
   over spring afternoons in the nineteenth century

while Marx in the library gloom
studies the birth rate of the weavers of Tilsit
and that gentle man Bakunin,
home after fingerfucking the countess,
applies his numb hands
to the making of bombs.

For Chekhov

Maryushka the beekeeper's
widow,
though three years mad,

writes daily letters
to her son. Semyon tran-
scribes them. The pages

are smudged by his hands,
stained
with the dregs of tea:

"My dearest Vanushka,
Sofia Aggrapina's ill
again. The master

asks for you. Wood
is dear. The cold
is early. Poor

Sofia Aggrapina!
The foreign doctor
gave her salts

but Semyon says her icon
candle guttered
St. John's eve. I am afraid,

Vanushka. When she's ill,
the master likes to have
your sister flogged.

She means no harm.
The rye is grey
this time of year.

When it is bad, Vanushka,
I go into the night
and the night eats me."

Two Views of Buson

1

A French scholar says he affected the Chinese manner.
When he took his friends into the countryside
To look at blossoms, they all saw Chinese blossoms.
He dressed accordingly and wept for the wild geese of
    Shosho.

2

One year after making love through the short
    midsummer night
He walked home at dawn and noticed that the river Oi
Had sunk two feet. The following year was better.
He saw bubbles of crab-froth among the river reeds.

After the Gentle Poet Kobayashi Issa

New Year's morning—
everything is in blossom!
I feel about average.

A huge frog and I
staring at each other,
neither of us moves.

This moth saw brightness
in a woman's chamber—
burned to a crisp.

Asked how old he was
the boy in the new kimono
stretched out all five fingers.

Blossoms at night,
like people
moved by music

Napped half the day;
no one
punished me!

Fiftieth birthday:

From now on,
it's all clear profit,
every sky.

Don't worry, spiders,
I keep house
   casually.

These sea slugs,
they just don't seem
   Japanese.

Hell:

Bright autumn moon;
pond snails crying
   in the saucepan.

Basho: A Departure

Summer is over and
we part, like eyelids,
like clams opening.

The Return of Robinson Jeffers

1

He shuddered briefly and stared down the long valley
    where the headland rose
And the lean gum trees rattled in the wind above Point
    Sur;
Alive, he had littered the mind's coast
With ghosts of Indians and granite and the dead fleshed
Bodies of desire. That work was done
And, whether done well or not, it had occupied him
As the hawks and the sea were occupied.
Now he could not say what brought him back.
He had imagined resurrection once: the lover of a woman
Who lived lonely in a little ranch house up the ridge
Came back, dragged from the grave by her body's need
To feel under ashen cloud-skies and in the astonishments
Of sunrise some truth beyond the daily lie
Of feeding absolute hunger the way a young girl might
    trap meadow mice
To feed a red-tailed hawk she kept encaged. She
    wanted to die once
As the sun dies in pure fire on the farthest sea-swells.
She had had enough and more of nights when the brain
Flickered and dissolved its little constellations and
    the nerves
Performed their dumb show in the dark among the
    used human smells of bedsheets.
So she burned and he came, a ghost in khaki and
    stunned skin,
And she fled with him. He had imagined, though he
    had not written,

The later moment in the pasture, in moonlight like pale
    stone,
When she lay beside him with an after-tenderness in all
    her bones,
Having become entirely what she was, though aware
    that the thing
Beside her was, again, just so much cheese-soft flesh
And jellied eye rotting in the pools of bone.
Anguish afterwards perhaps, but he had not thought
    afterwards.
Human anguish made him cold.
He told himself the cries of men in war were no more
    conscious
Nor less savage than the shrill repetitions of the Steller's
    jay
Flashing through live oaks up Mal Paso Canyon
And that the oaks, rooted and growing toward their
    grace,
Were—as species go—
More beautiful.

2

He had given himself to stone gods.
I imagine him thinking of that woman
While a live cloud of gulls
Plumes the wind behind a trawler
Throbbing toward the last cannery at Monterey.
The pelicans are gone which had, wheeling,
Written Chinese poems on the sea. The grebes are gone
That feasted on the endless hunger of the flashing runs
Of salmon. And I imagine that he saw, finally,
That though rock stands, it does not breed.
He feels specific rage. Feels, obscurely, that his sex
Is his, not god-force only, but his own soft flesh grown
    thick

With inconsolable desire. The grebes are gone.
He feels a plain man's elegiac tenderness,
An awkward brotherhood with the world's numb poor
His poems had despised. Rage and tenderness are pain.
He feels pain as rounding at the hips, as breasts.
Pain blossoms in his belly like the first dark
Stirrings of a child, a surfeit of the love that he had
    bled to rock
And twisted into cypress haunts above the cliffs.
He knows he has come back to mourn,
To grieve, womanish, a hundred patient years
Along this fragile coast. I imagine the sky's arch,
Cloud-swift, lifts him then, all ache in sex and breasts,
Beyond the leached ashes of dead fire,
The small jeweled hunger in the seabird's eye.

Measure

Recurrences.
Coppery light hesitates
again in the small-leaved

Japanese plum. Summer
and sunset, the peace
of the writing desk

and the habitual peace
of writing, these things
form an order I only

belong to in the idleness
of attention. Last light
rims the blue mountain

and I almost glimpse
what I was born to,
not so much in the sunlight

or the plum tree
as in the pulse
that forms these lines.

Applications of the Doctrine

That professor of French,
trying to start his car
among the innocent snowdrifts,
is the author of a famous book
on the self.

*

The self is probably an illusion
and language the structure of illusions.
The self is beguiled, anyway,
by this engine of thought.

*

The self shuffles cards
with absurd dexterity.
The deck includes
an infinite number
of one-eyed jacks.

*

On warm days
he knows he should marry Being,
a nice girl, steady
but relentless.

*

The self has agreed to lecture
before a psychoanalytic study group.
On the appointed day he
does not appear, thereby
meeting his obligation.

*

The self grants an audience
to the Pope.
They talk shop.

*

The snark is writing a novel
called *The Hunting of the Self*.
The self is composing a monograph
on the frames of antique mirrors.

*

The self botanizes.
He dreams of breeding, one day,
an odorless narcissus.

*

There is a girl the self loves.
She has been trying to study him for days
but her mind keeps
wandering.

*

The Pornographer

He has finished a day's work.
Placing his pencil in a marmalade jar
which is colored the soft grey
of a crumbling Chinese wall
in a Sierra meadow, he walks
from his shed into the afternoon
where orioles rise aflame from the orchard.
He likes the sun and he is tired
of the art he has spent on the brown starfish
anus of his heroine, the wet duck's-feather tufts
of armpit and thigh, tender and roseate enfoldings
of labia within labia, the pressure and darkness
and long sudden falls from slippery stone
in the minds of the men with anonymous tongues
in his book. When he relaxes, old images
return. He is probably in Central Asia.
Once again he is marched to the wall.
All the faces are impassive. Now
he is blinded. There is a long silence
in which he images clearly the endless sky
and the horizon, swift with cloud scuds.
Each time, in imagination, he attempts
to stand as calmly as possible
in what is sometimes morning warmth,
sometimes evening chill.

The Pornographer, Melancholy

Summer is over and his friends are gone—
vanished as inexplicably
    as the pearly fluids
which gushed from sporting ladies
    in the novels of a hundred years before.

The leaves of the plane tree
    brown and curl, the world
tenses in the early cold toward final
    literal insistences: autumn,
death, the cold comfort of reason
    and clitoral orgasm. In the day's work
he married two seven-sided orgies
    in a ceremony as delicate and involuted
as copulating octopi,
                    wafting pale purple
    hedges of sea heather.

His friends are gone and he is reflective.
    The essence of seasons is repetition.
They die and shine, die and shine.

The Pornographer at the End of Winter

He had thought March was the blackbird's month.
   April is the blackbird's month.
They lord it in the trees. Their cries
   are the seasonal delectation.

He leaves off the defoliation of drugged virgins
   to read calligraphies of pheasant tracks
in the last crisp snow around the soggy fields.
   Some buds, magenta-colored, green-veined,
sap rising.

There is a high windy vault of sky & precise
   two-note whistles from a cardinal
repeat at intervals and thin to the shape
   of leafless trees along the forest edge.
Very soon he is cold. Eyes watery with light,

   he hurries toward the house,
bored by the frail white body, coltish, slack
   among cushions he hasn't colored yet.
He breathes muddy April, imagines
   limbs akimbo, small swart hairs.

All around him is the gravel music
   of the blackbirds' cries.

Politics of a Pornographer

Like America, his art consists
in the absence of scale. He is no less
mad, but his Oedipus
meets, always, at the crossroads
his mother and trembles in the sun.
The dust is mallow
and the light is mallow-brown.
In his mind there are only
a summer meadow, breasts,
the mossy tuft, his cock,
and twining legs.
There is no walled city come to.
The sphinx proposes nothing.
There is no plague.

In Weather

The Failure of Buffalo to Levitate

Millard Fillmore died here.
His round body is weighted by marble angels.
He lies among the great orators of the Iroquois.

Paint does not arrest the tradebook houses
in their elegant decay. They peel like lizards
in the dying avenues of elm.

Gentle enough, night drifts
above the yellow bursts of aspen in the park.
Something innocent and reptilian

suffers here, cumbrously.
The souls of the wives of robber barons
are imprisoned in the chandeliers.

House

Quick in the April hedge
   were juncos and kinglets.
I was at the window
   just now, the bacon
sizzled under hand,
   the coffee steamed
fragrantly & fountains
   of the Water Music
issued from another room.
   Living in a house
we live in the body
   of our lives, last night
the odd after-dinner light
   of early spring & now
the sunlight warming or
   shadowing the morning rooms.

I am conscious of being
   myself the inhabitant
of certain premises:
   coffee & bacon & Handel
& upstairs asleep my wife.
   Very suddenly
old dusks break over me,
   the thick shagged heads
of fig trees near the fence
   & not wanting to go in
& swallows looping
   on the darkened hill

& all that terror
  in the house
& barely, only barely,
  a softball
falling toward me
  like a moon.

After I Seized the Pentagon

Washington was calm, murderous, neo-classical.
More lies than cherry trees and nothing changed.
And drowsing home through northern Pennsylvania
the dawn light fooled me. Dreams. We talked
and, half-asleep, my body hummed. We were too
    excited.
After dark searchlights had cast troopers
in huge shadow on penitential stone. I saw
two shadows raising clubs to beat a girl,
a sickness in my stomach and a worse one in my head,
a pleased sense of historical drama, of the aesthetics
of evil. We were too excited. Eyes open, eyes closed,
I saw frost bleach the hills to western grass
and dreamed of small-breasted girls,
jack cheese, the smell of sweat, the acrid
smell of sage. Hiking, and morning woke me
to a maple blaze.
        I thought of pepper trees,
survivors, modest local gods, tough-barked,
of an easy grace and bitter fruit
which grow in riven country near the sea
where spring is clement and the land an aftermath.

Assassin

In Arcata, California
north on the fog-and-clapboard coast
the bronze statue of McKinley
stands, empty-handed, in the village square.
His green corroded arms outstretched
it is not clear whether the former President
embraces the Pacific or weeps
that there are no more distances
a man can thrust a railroad through.
Here in Buffalo the body of his assassin lies,
humus dreaming of life after death
and the green republic. Ring-necked
pheasants peck about his grave
in the old pastoral cemetery.
Their dark eyes gleam
as light, dying,
refracts in the polluted air.

Counterpane:
Grandfather's Death

On the pillow
the embroidered flowers
are fading
fading that patient spider
my grandmother

who made the best
of losses
bright quilts from rags
that are every bird
Audubon ever killed
in America.

In Weather

   What I wanted
in the pearly repetitions of February
was vision. All winter,
grieved and dull,
I hungered for it.
Sundays I looked for lightning-
stricken trees
in the slow burning of the afternoon
to cut them down, split
the dry centers,
and kindle from their death
an evening's warmth
in the uxorius amber repetitions
of the house. Dusks
weighted me, the fire,
the dim trees. I saw
the bare structure
of their hunger for light
reach to where darkness
joined them. The dark
and the limbs tangled
luxuriant as hair.
I could feel night gather them
but removed my eyes from the tug of it
and watched the fire,
a smaller thing,
contained by the hewn stone
of the dark hearth.

2

    I can't decide
about my garbage and the creatures
who come at night to root
and scatter it. I could lock it
in the shed, but I imagine
wet noses, bodies grown alert
to the smells of warm decay
in the cold air. It seems a small thing
to share what I don't want,
but winter mornings the white yard
blossoms grapefruit peels,
tin cans, plastic bags,
the russet cores of apples.
The refuse of my life
surrounds me and the sense of waste
in the dreary gathering of it
compels me all the more
to labor for the creatures
who quiver and are quick-eyed
and bang the cans at night
and are not grateful. The other morning,
walking early in the new sun,
I was rewarded. A thaw turned up
the lobster shells from Christmas eve.
They rotted in the yard
and standing in the muddy field I caught,
as if across great distances,
a faint rank fragrance of the sea.

3

    There are times
I wish my ignorance were
more complete. I remember
clamming inland beaches
on the January tides
along Tomales Bay. A raw world
where green crabs
which have been exposed
graze nervously on intertidal kelp
and sea anemones are clenched and colorless
in eddying pools
near dumb clinging starfish
on the sides and undersides of rock.
Among the cockles and the horseneck clams,
I turned up long, inch-thick
sea worms. Female,
phallic, ruddy brown, each one
takes twenty years to grow.
Beach people call them *innkeepers*
because the tiny male lives inside
and feeds on plankton
in the water that the worm
churns through herself to move.
I watched the brown things
that brightness bruised
writhing in the sun. Then,
carefully, I buried them.
And, eyes drifting, heart-
sick, honed to the wind's edge,
my mind became the male
drowsing in that inland sea
who lives in darkness,
drops seed twice in twenty years,
and dies. I look from my window
to the white fields
and think about the taste of clams.

4

A friend, the other night,
read poems full of rage
against the poor uses of desire
in mere enactment. A cruel music
lingered in my mind.
The poems made me think
I understood
why men cut women up. Hating
the source, nerved,
irreducible, that music hacked
the body till the source was gone.
Then the heavy cock wields,
rises, spits seed
at random and the man
shrieks, homeless
and perfected in the empty dark.
His god is a thrust of infinite desire
beyond the tame musk
of companionable holes.
It descends to women occasionally
with contempt and languid tenderness.
I tried to hate my wife's cunt,
the sweet place where I rooted,
to imagine the satisfied disgust
of cutting her apart,
bloody and exultant
in the bad lighting and scratchy track
of butcher shops
in short experimental films.
It was easier than I might have supposed.
o spider cunt, o raw devourer.
I wondered what to make
of myself. There had been a thaw.
I looked for green shoots
in the garden, wild flowers in the woods.
I found none.

5

In March the owls
began to mate. Moon
on windy snow. Mournful,
liquid, the dark hummed
their cries, a soft
confusion. Hard frost
feathered the windows.
I could not sleep.
I imagined the panic
of the meadow mouse,
the star-nosed mole.
Slowly at first, I
made a solemn face
and tried the almost human wail
of owls, ecstatic
in the winter trees, *twoo*, *twoo*.
I drew long breaths.
My wife stirred in our bed.
Joy seized me.

6

Days return
day to me, the brittle light.
My alertness has no
issue. Deep in the woods
starburst needles of the white pine
are roof to the vacancies
in standing still. Wind
from the lake stings me.
Hemlocks grow cerebral
and firm in the dim attenuation
of the afternoon. The longer
dusks are a silence
born in pale redundancies
of silence. Walking home
I follow the pawprints of the fox.
I know that I know myself
no more than a seed
curled in the dark of a winged pod
knows flourishing.

Letter

I had wanted to begin
by telling you I saw another
tanager below the pond
where I had sat for half an hour
feeding on wild berries
in the little clearing near the pines
that hide the lower field
and then looked up from red berries
to the quick red bird brilliant
in the light. I have seen
more yarrow and swaying
Queen Anne's lace around the woods
as hawkweed and nightshade
wither and drop seed. A new blue flower,
sweet, yellow-stamened, ovary inferior,
has recently sprung up.
                          But I had the odd
feeling, walking to the house
to write this down, that I had left
the birds and flowers in the field,
rooted or feeding. They are not in my
head, are not now on this page.
It was very strange to me, but I think
their loss was your absence. I wanted
to be walking up with Leif, the sun
behind us skipping off the pond,
the windy maple sheltering the house,
and find you there and say
here! a new blue flower (ovary inferior)

and busy Leif and Kris with naming
in a world I love. You even have
my field guide. It's you I love.
I have believed so long
in the magic of names and poems.
I hadn't thought them bodiless
at all. Tall Buttercup. Wild Vetch.
"Often I am permitted to return
to a meadow." It all seemed real to me
last week. Words. You are the body
of my world, root and flower, the
brightness and surprise of birds.
I miss you, love. Tell Leif
you're the names of things.

Lament for the Poles of Buffalo

For Margaret and Leslie Fiedler

1

These green New York summers—
foreign and magical to me
as novels were when,
younger, I read long afternoons
of seedling and ripe harvest, marshes
where your masters hunted snipe,
sloe and *zubrowka* gathered from the fields
to scent their vodka. There was snow
and deep spring seepage
that heaved green through three hot months
in the four olive volumes of *The Peasants*
by Ladislas Reymont. They had not
much likeness to my Coast Range hills,
tawny with wild oat, or the valley farms
brown-bodied in the August heat.
You were twice-translated. English
for a music I had never heard,
rain for snow, teal and canvasback for snipe.

Now my eye finds you
where brown haze dissolves
the lucid sky, lakeward and riverward.
Smokestacks, steel, threads of smoke westering.
I think these days of Esterhazy
and his serfs. Up here it is intensely green,
suburban. I follow muskrat paths
toward streams along the meadow

where bittersweet nightshade grows
violet-thick. Yellow pistils
dart from the petals like tiny tongues.
The ovaries swell lazily
toward pale sepals on the underside.
He owned a hundred thousand Polish souls,
Esterhazy, Haydn's patron.
Catherine of Russia gave him
twenty thousand once, men and women,
because he had such grace in flattery.
Mr. Lewandowski, Mrs. Slominski,
I toss hard words at you
from here on Chestnut Ridge,
white Anglo-Saxon words,
heavy, strange as buckshot
on the tongues of your grandfathers.

2

When Elias Crockett hauled
his life up narrow canyons of the Genesee,
a pair of huge, gentle, brown-eyed oxen
bore the load: wife, tools, a millstone.
He settled on Lake Erie's northeast shore.
Buffalo Creek was low in early fall. He unyoked,
unpacked, and one of the beasts
he butchered on the spot
and very agreeably ate. There was no
unkindness in it—they were not
his kind. Flames leaped
to lick the marbled crusts of fat.
The thick steaks were incense in the air.
Your families came later
from coal pits and burrows of Pennsylvania
looking for work above the ground.
Their eyes adjusted, briefly, to the light.
Crockett owned the general store.

3

I testified last week
before your grand jury.
They wanted me to name
your children's names.
In a building full of classical
representations of justice
and various insignia of the not
quite extinct Iroquois. Old fears:
if the Easter candle is extinguished,
the buckwheat will not grow.
Never slice a melon on the Baptist's day.
Beware the blood-dark mark
that stains the breasts of Jews.
They asked me for the names of Jews,
now that English vowels in your mouths
are nasalized, at home,
flat as pellets doctors dug
out of students' skulls last spring.
Bitter, they rose up
against the war they've watched you wear
proudly these five years
like Pan Master's cast-off coat.

So summer comes again.
The elms in full leaf
imitate cathedrals as we planned,
the sick elms. You plan Free Eastern Europe Day
these desperate evenings
when the Sunday *New York Times*
seems thinner than the air and less alive
with the communicable anguish
and boredom of cities.
I wander in the woods
like the literary peasants
of the nineteenth century

who, for eternity, will gather
mushrooms in the forests of Lithuania
at dawn. Mickiewicz, your epic poet,
describes each fungus
by its wineglass shape, recalls
the clear fragile crystal
whose cold touch the horny fingers
of your forebears never knew,
morels for burgundy,
and for champagne the pale upswept cups
of chanterelles.

4

I dreamed this dream:
of late winter at Crystal Beach
where the old amusement park
is dying like the lake.
A wilderness
of huge frozen drifts of snow.
We ran, my son and I,
toward harder ice
in long blue shadows from the early sun,
sinking and clambering.
Out as far as it was safe to go,
an old woman and her husband
bundled there in coarse grey wool
were sitting on a tarp. She
spoke to me in Polish
or Russian. I knew
who she was but I couldn't say.
We were at the edge of things.
Pointing west toward deep water
and the point, she smiled
and spoke again. Her eyes welled tears
against the cold. We looked.
White over white soaring,

churned water, grey, blue-grey,
and just above, in swarms,
gulls, golden-eyes, and mute fantastic swans.

The next day I remembered
who she was: Grushenka.
This was their dream if they escaped,
America. I knew
when I first read *The Brothers Karamazov*,
eighteen years old and on another coast,
that they had come, that their great heat
burned here. I didn't wonder then
what they had come to. I have
loved your ancestors
in books. The peasants of Europe
stirred there and sang
and killed. Summer meadows
of an old wisdom, our communal guilt,
forgiveness, new justice, and the black earth.
There was dawn sun on snow
and the children, remembering
their dead ones, cried, "Hurrah!"

5

Still the old servility.
You don't even own the city
where the landlord lets you play
at politics. It is not your wealth
that gathers to a foulness in the air.
Your shit and their sludge commingle
in the lake, married in dead salmon
and poisoned roe. Only the houses.
I have come to like the houses,
warm against winter, slack-jawed
in summer as they settle on the lawns,
new sphinxes of the riddle

of sheer bulk. Evenings life
issues from them and nights the lights
go out in windows
down the block. I have a friend
who says he pities you at night,
thinking of the Catholic church
and all the dirty books in corners
of the corner stores. And I am sorry
that you suffer joy in shame.
It was not so in the poets.
They envied your bodies. They envied
your marriage to a land
they merely owned. They feared and hungered,
knowing that you would, one day, rise up.

6

This patriotism: commissioners
of bad streets, a grubby park.
I notice there's no statue there
of Stiff-arm George. Even the history
of this city breeds
a comic opera melancholy
like some poor poet's life.
Stiff-arm George was the Seneca
who wandered into Buffalo,
ponderously drunk, a day in 1802
and stabbed two white men,
whittlers, on the trading office steps.
George was arrested, the loafers
from the steps were tended to,
and a garrison from Fort Niagara
was stationed here. Law and order.
The settlers flocked in. Crockett
throve. But not before

Red Jacket, the Cato of the Iroquois,
had led his braves to town
and delivered a defense. He
talked eight hours in the sun,
marshaling his periods
in a tongue no white man
this side of Montreal could understand.
Your founding father, Stiff-arm George, was hanged.

7
He still lives here.
He is your sons. Bored or at war,
they wander through the streets.
They want Lake Erie's shore and peace.
They wear your pride, justice and black earth,
and you do not forgive. They dream of Indians
as the landlords and poets of Poland
dreamed of you. It is an ancient
imagination and it begets,
this order with the random symmetries
of mallow poppies in the field,
the dying and green leafing of the grass,
meadows crackling in the midday heat,
alive with seed. It translates easily.